Can you hear the a sound in the middle of the words sad, bag, van, fan, and ham?

Here is a cat. What is the cat looking for? He is looking for a rat.

Can you say the words cat and rat?

THIS IS THE LETTER e

The letter e makes the first sound in the word elephant.

The engine is going into the entrance of the tunnel.

Say these words and listen carefully for the e sound. Where does the e sound come in each word? Does it come at the beginning or in the middle?

web

jet

men

elbow

egg

Which letter makes the sound at the beginning of the words engine, entrance, and exit?

THIS IS THE LETTER i

Oops! Someone has spilled the ink.
Can you hear the sound at the
beginning of the word ink?
The letter i makes that sound.

Do the words
ink and
insect begin
with the
same sound?

One word below does not begin with an i
sound. Where does the i sound come
in this word?

zipper

instrument

invitation

Say the words pig, dig, and pit.
Can you hear the i sound in the
middle of these words?

Do these words have
the same sound in the
middle? Listen as you
say them.

Lid

fish

pin

THIS IS THE LETTER

The names of these animals all begin with the same sound. Can you say the names?

ostrich

octopus

The letter o makes the first sound in all of these names.

otter

Can you see what these shapes are?

top

rod

dog

doll

One of these animals has an o sound in the middle. Which is it?

bird

frog

duck

THIS IS THE LETTER u

Can you see the umbrella?
It is upside down.

The letter u makes the sound at the
beginning of umbrella and upside down.

Look at the ugly bugs.
Which bug is upset?
Which bug is unwell?
Which bug is unhappy?